# We Borrowed Gentleness

# WE BORROWED
# GENTLENESS

# J. ESTANISLAO LOPEZ

**Alice James Books**
NEW GLOUCESTER, ME
alicejamesbooks.org

10 9 8 7 6 5 4 3 2 1

Alice James Books are published by Alice James Poetry Cooperative, Inc.

Alice James Books
Auburn Hall
60 Pineland Drive, Suite 206
New Gloucester, ME 04260
www.alicejamesbooks.org

Library of Congress Cataloging-in-Publication Data

Names: Lopez, J. Estanislao, author.
Title: We borrowed gentleness / J. Estanislao Lopez.
Description: New Gloucester, ME : Alice James Books, [2022]
Identifiers: LCCN 2022018214 (print) | LCCN 2022018215 (ebook) | ISBN
   9781948579285 (trade paperback) | ISBN 9781948579377 (epub)
Subjects: LCGFT: Poetry.
Classification: LCC PS3612.O623 W4 2022  (print) | LCC PS3612.O623
(ebook)
   | DDC 811/.6--dc23/eng/20220413
LC record available at https://lccn.loc.gov/2022018214
LC ebook record available at https://lccn.loc.gov/2022018215

Alice James Books gratefully acknowledges support from individual do-
nors, private foundations, the National Endowment for the Arts, and the
Amazon Literary Partnership. Funded in part by a grant from the Maine
Arts Commission, an independent state agency supported by the National
Endowment for the Arts.

 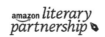 

Cover art by Yanin Ruibal

# CONTENTS

*For Dorothy,*
*For Astacia*

## A METAPHOR

You raise a glass of iced water to your lips.
Feeling a strange touch,
you look into the glass to find
a dead gnat floating at the surface.
There are metaphors everywhere
for the presence of evil.
But metaphors are misread.
Too late, you learn
that evil is not signified by the gnat,
a casualty, but by the water,
which we raise to our lips every single day.

## INDEPENDENCE DAY IN WEST TEXAS

Bought with the soiled coins
I pinched from the floorboard of our father's truck,
my sister's sparkler fell into her sandal.

Below her body,
light pooled against desert night—

a coincidence of beauty and suffering,
which I would learn is an old coincidence.

Old, too, a boy's hands placed
on the causal chain.

My mother smothered the glowing lace,
first with her hands,
then with a towel my brother fetched.

Fireworks continued.

Horned lizards skittered beneath wood pallets.
I sunk behind our Dodge, and, as my sister cried out

to a luminous sky I then believed was listening,
I buried my legs in gravel,
counting seconds between its shifts of hue.

After the fireworks, gunfire resounded,
continuing through my sleep. I dreamt explosions
turning milky, flooding the desert,

saturating it—

our feet steeped in the milk, my sister's and mine
together. Then, others' feet: our countrymen,

who pledged this precise disaster:
that for her woundedness she'd be remembered,

for her woundedness she'd be loved.

## LITTLE WORDS

Every year, the script of hatred
grows more legible inside me.

I can feel the letters' edges
harden into a strange cartilage.

Sold off for marriage at the age of thirteen,
my great-grandmother never said
that she hated her father,

who wed their survival
to her mouth's conscription.

My mother, in retelling the story, recommits to it.

There were the breadlines, the suicides.

Misery grows on an inverted tree—
its perfume releasing
with each broken husk of family.

Take view of my mother who could never escape my father.

Take view of my great-grandmother's crucifix,
which she prayed beneath,
and beneath the surface of her prayer
was a hatred of God, unutterable, so passed down quietly like a
    gene.

Take view of the spurs on those little words,
*Te amo, I love you,*

and test their prick, whetted by contradiction,
on your own tongue.

Ask how much taking is enough.

## THE CONTRACT

He had shaken our hands earlier on the jobsite,
but now would not pay my father for our work.

Through the truck's open window, my right ear
caught the steely whistle of a passing train's friction

against the rails, while my left listened to my father
dial a number repeatedly. A broken air conditioner

blew lukewarm air into the hot cab. This wasn't
his first time being cheated, nor would it be the last.

That smile with which the contractor met me, how
securely fastened it seemed to its frame—his hand's

warmth, liver spots a constellation full of good luck.
My English had impressed him, as it did others

who gave my father work. And my father, too,
taught me *work* that way, as if it were a gift

one might open on Christmas morning beneath
ornamental dust, a gift that could adorn the walls

of the widening gap between my father and that man—
unbridgeable, I learned that day. In conversation,

before we hung a single drywall panel to a stud,
they fabricated nostalgia for a misremembered past.

*The Good Old Days*, where—they pretended—
they could have broken bread. I could not ask

my father if he blamed himself, so I assigned him
blame. He had insisted on a verbal contract,

a handshake, a pact made of air, shared
between one man and another like        laughter.

## PROMISE

Ice melts into the glass.
My mother laughs a laugh that pours around us
like overdrawn bathwater.
The nearest table asks to be moved.
Outside the restaurant, banana leaves drip rain
into freshly shoveled mulch.
When she topples one salt-rimmed glass,
the waiter brings her another.
Such reckless joy—
her answer to the agenda of forfeiture
set before her
by her parents, her husband,
her children.

When I was a boy,
she held my injured leg
in her muscular hands,
rubbing away my soreness,
and spoke of a future
in which I would lift her
from poverty.
Her son, the doctor.
Her son, the architect.
I promised her, then
and again each time
she asked, too young
to understand the anesthesia
of a promise
that readies the flesh
of the coming years
for the scalpel—in whose
unsteady hands if not my own—

## THE POLITICS OF RIVERS

On its brittle vine,
     my grandfather's voice ripened with stories
          he thought forgotten.

The time he gashed his elbow on the tracks.
     The time a boy overturned an altar of votive candles,
          almost igniting the church.

The time he stole a wrestling figurine
     from the town market only to have it stolen from him.
          From the windows of his childhood home,

I could see the cemetery,
     and beyond his father's headstone,
          construction lights glowed.

Drills shrieked like children, tin-tongued.
     A Walmart's steel frame incited local youth,
          whose chants I could only parse

the music of.
     The desperate snuck on-site,
          working shovels, haggling afterward for pay.

In the house, creatures scratched the night's percussion.
     Half-dreamt ants hauled off slivers of leftover bread.
          I awoke

to my grandfather's mumbling
     in the adjacent room. My brothers lay beside me.
          I felt homesickness unfurling

from my gut as a spangled sadness.
     A longing so sure of its direction—toward
          the river that marches

according to its nature, down the path
    of least resistance—
        giving freely its terrible advice.

## LET'S NOT GET CARRIED AWAY

by the officers dressed
in our permission.
If we find ourselves
getting carried away,
let's remember the forefathers'
prescience, having killed
one another off.
When a president
says barbed wire
can be a beautiful sight,
the words carry the weight
of history. General Scott,
having occupied Mexico,
confessed that his soldiers
committed horrors *sufficient*
*to make heaven weep*.
Some soldiers
bottled that celestial brine,
viscous and shimmering,
carried vials home
to nurse their children.
Today, we drink with children
of those children. So drink,
but remember yourself.
Remember, too, how young
this nation is.
Drink to the carrion
paved over with war memorials.
Never forget how cruel
children can be.

## THEODICY WRITTEN IN THE OCCUPIED SANDS

We should not have been surprised

at the gardener's bloodthirst
once family was lost to the fight.

Asters went unwatered except by rain.

It may not have been prayer caught in our throat
but privilege, or cartilage, or birds.

There are things we did not imagine:

cities bloused in ruin;
an enduring, flammable night.

There are things that we ignore:

lands razed by God's disinterest;

an old historian pointing to a wound
convinced it spills not blood, but light.

## DIÁSPORA

I am losing my brother to whiteness.
At family dinners, I sit beside his apparition
that still makes a chewing sound.
My ear up to his heart, I hear it beating
*patriot, patriot*—misplaced stress and a beat too long.

Even more worrisome
are his patterns of speech.

As if the two syllables consecrate
the air around him,
the lineage behind him,
he says the word at every chance: *legal,*
pointing to our father, who gives a solemn nod.

I am losing my brother
to a whiteness he's convinced
will bestow what his father couldn't.

He speaks of pride and birthrights.
He speaks of gristle
that must be worked through
to enjoy the brightness of bone.

I love my brother.

I love my brother
the way I was taught
to love my enemies.

He finishes his meal and lays
his hand on my shoulder, saying
that if I would just love my country
the way he does, I'd be a better citizen—

I'd feel connected to the land.

## ALTERNATE ENDING: SOLOMON'S MISJUDGMENT

No one calls Solomon wise after seeing the child split
between the two claimants. The flesh returned

to two beds. Neither party is satisfied, but both know
the other is dissatisfied, and there's a certain satisfaction

there. Solomon complains about human nature
to his dozen nearest wives. *Is this my blessed nation?*

he cries as one wife shepherds her children out of sight,
knowing better than anyone the scent of divine whim approaching.

After wiping off his sword, Solomon hears the voice of God
like the clinks of a belt loosening. But it's his own belt.

He was never his father's favorite. His ivory throne
now smells faintly of iron, of all the old wars.

He misses his brother, beautiful Absalom, whose hair
still hangs in a tree. Coarse flower. Absalom, abloom.

## LAREDO DUPLEX

Across the river, Nuevo Laredo. My father,
born there, was born on one side of defeat.

> Born there, and he crossed sides—defeat
> trailed him, ghost-like, with a river's hush.

His paper trail: ghost-like; a river hushed
under El Norte's second name, the South.

> A war of second names pushed us south.
> Another war pushed us north, again.

(Another war: to push and push against
such profanation of the body.)

> There are countless ways to profane a body—
> I won't recount them here.

I won't recount them. Here,
across the river: Nuevo Laredo. My father.

## THE OFFERING

In Herrán's *La ofrenda*, an old man's body flags
in the back of a punt that hauls marigolds to be left
on gravesites. No mouth opens to speak, and a small girl
gazes directly into a century she will never touch.
Water darkens the canvas to its invisible core,
encasing the flowers' loud light in impossibility.

In my grandfather's den, a garland of marigolds drapes
across the window, trembling from an a/c unit's hum.
In the corner, he sits bare-chested and drowsy,
his stitches running like water down his body. I wince
at the sound his chest must have made, cracked open
in the warmth of a surgical lamp. My father talks to him

with a low voice in their second tongue. There's music to it:
*Blood sugar, blood sugar*—my grandfather nods slightly
and waves my father away, annoyed by his breath.
After all the talk of building something new in this country,
my grandfather's body fails the same way as his own father's.
His life conforms as he feared it would, the way a petal

in a bushel of flowers is subsumed into bothersome
brightness. What good is beauty that rests so namelessly?
My father rubs his father's feet, easing him into rest,
his hands gentler than I'd ever known. He turns to me
with eyes like that girl on the punt, exhausted
by the centuries he'll exist as, at best, an absence.

Both of them afraid that their names will amount
to no more than engraving on a plate that a stranger
mows around. They wonder who will leave them flowers.
They look at me. They look at me and have reason to doubt.

## PATTERNS

I fold my latest pay stub
into an origami lily
and rest it on my father's chest.

In the yard, my father and I gathered
pecans as we did every fall—my bag, torn
at the bottom. His, filling with sand.

*Let us call to mind our sins.*
The three nails that, in boyhood, pierced
my feet adorn His mouth like teeth.

Physics lesson: dark hair, mine,
absorbs light and releases it
as heat, feeding entropy.

Lying in the truck bed, I pretended to sleep.
A dog raged behind a fence. My parents' yelling,
muffled into music by window glass.

Physics lesson: sound
is kinetic energy involving
movement, heat, loss.

I touch my own throat, warm
from my raised voice. My son weeps.
Wind shoves sand from a dune's crest.


*Inheritance*, the scientist says,
can be sequenced. Science, his father says,
*excuses no one from their ghosts.*


My father's hair, fragrant as the desert.
The one Christ might have wandered,
talking to (he feared) himself.

## A MIRACLE

How the small griefs multiply

like loaves in a basket touched

by a god who insists we remain

where we are, who insists

that with this we be fed.

## ELEGY IN THE ABSENCE OF ANSWERS

There's a hidden economy:

       the way bitterness compounds on itself;

my own purchase of estrangement.

When a wing breaks on a window,
       the world has one more burden

to commodify. I'd argue with those that say suffering
is capital,

but its accruement of interest is palpable on the tongues
of many whom I love.

       I, too, was lied to
about the morning's erasure of the night.

       The bodies remain buried.
Their deaths remain unanswered by the police and God.

       One creature of grief turns that pain,

all that rage,
       into a second, beating heart,

and because it asks,
       I lay my head on its breast and listen.

## MY UNCLE'S KILLER

wipes spots of toothpaste from the bathroom mirror
he shares nightly with his son. There, he's humanized

again in my imagination, which keeps endowing him
with other forms: a lion panting gun smoke;

a scythe-shaped smile on a child's back. Can I tell you
that sometimes I utter the word *justice* and mean *revenge*?

On my best nights, I mean mercy, but my best
is my rarest form. The figure of my uncle's blood

on the pavement, lit faintly by a gas station sign,
never changes. It's always, in my imagination, that same

dark isthmus connecting his body to the storm drain.
It floods in this city every year. In the last one,

several coffins escaped their graves to the horror
of almost everyone. I'm glad to see the past intrude

as spectacle, an image captivating our flighty memory.
Freedom, after all, is what binds me to the worst version

of myself. Shout, *Freedom*. You can't help it.
You've made a threat.

## PORVENIR

Against a dense wall of desert night

fifteen kidnapped men and boys

strained their eyes.

Behind them, rifles glowed honey-orange in torchlight—
soldiers' rifles, each pointed through their bodies,
toward the same Texan sky my father would,

in fifty years, cross a river to sleep beneath.

That sound I hear every Fourth of July
parenthesizing fireworks,
the ellipsis after, gunshots
aimed at the past or the future,
indifferent

that's the sound their families heard,
that's the sound they wept at.

Wounds caked in winter sand,

their bodies were hauled back across the river,

buried far from the settlement they'd named

Porvenir—a future

the Anglo soldiers razed, false reports

drawn with usual flourish and detail:

*Bandits. Fired upon.*

I wonder about the ashes,

if still some are carried by wind across a soldier's lips,

up into his nostrils,
as he mouths commands to refugees trapped again
in this valley where each hour drags

lightless revelation

strung to the promise of its return.

Like other soldiers, he writes home not knowing
to ask for forgiveness, his forgiveness already
a rumor that spreads from grave to unmarked
grave, from town to ghost town, over land that knows
arid is the weather of his forgiveness.

From this parched soil, shoots of memory grow
into fields touched more by wind than scythe.

(Within each image is a contract.

My father signed our names—
his pen, my tongue.

He spoke to us in English
about the future.

But the past—
*I got us here. That should be enough.*)

I hear the narrative of descent from what this country was
to what it is becoming

and hear our feet on shifting gravel, shoveled earth—

as if the future hadn't already been burned,

as if we were headed toward, what, absolution?

Nothing dissolves;

the desert preserves too much.

## THE NEW REGIME

Dogma sweetens the air like spring wind.
Strawberry fields ripen in the countryside,
and birds, singing, have no idea to whom they sing.

What I love most about the change of regime
is how it resets our metaphors. Who's to say
what can be gotten away with, now?

Clouds, rolling across the sky with the elegance
of an indictment, name me a co-conspirator—
and who am I to doubt the clouds?

I insist that I am no one. A mote of dust
on the framework. I insist it mere
coincidence—those zealots starting fires,

my little body staying warm.

## THE FRAMEWORK OF AN IMAGINARY NATION

*First, we imagined a wager*
*against our survival. We said damned if we do,*
*damned if we don't—so we did.*
*At some point, we were the underdogs,*
*and that underdoggedness swaddles us still*
*against each cold threshold of conscience.*
*Yes, we dressed our dead in the satin*
*of the Latinate. We pointed*
*vaguely to some old texts,*
*and everyone's devotion burned brightly,*
*collective swamp lights*
*silhouetting cypress. We said democracy's*
*spread is a natural consequence.*
*A law of metaphysics! We said the gods*
*of this nation don't parse the votive*
*and the vote. Now, we've been accused*
*of standing by these values.*
*And to our accusers we say,*
*why not be the bigger person?*
*You can wave your flags*
*a little lower. It was never our intention*
*that these monuments*
*to our achievement also serve*
*as the only markers of your graves.*

## LIKE IT IS

It's easy to be liked
when you tell it like it is.

When you say our tanks in the streets dazzle us
not with their beauty, but effectiveness.

No, not *our* streets.

When you say the apple falls not far
from the tree's noose.

The student who planted it says it was just a joke,
and his mother breathes a white sigh of relief.

I consume the bird that consumed the beetle
whose larvae feasts beneath cemetery grass,

that's how it is. Some people die with a mouthful
of the earth's riches; others, with plain-salted fear.

When you're direct, people respect that.
And respect keeps you safe when law fails

or conspires against you. It's someone's job
to polish the valves poisoning the sky, the earth, the children.

Sometimes, *ours*.

The job gets done—proudly, even. That's
how it is. See how easily the words

give shape to the unspeakable?
It—is. Say it. Say it is.

## ALTERNATE ENDING: THE UNRECORDED
## BITTERNESS OF ABRAHAM

Let me return to God not as a believer
but as a member of the jury. O Repeat Offender,

I cannot profess Your benevolence, again.
Let me return to God with a rock-keened knife

and opportunity. Let no angel, this time, stop me.
My son describes his faith as stronger than before.

While lighting the sacrificial fire, I thumbed
the chopped wood's grain—I've kept with me

a splinter. No, the boy who walked home
with me was no longer my son, but an effigy.

Let the promise of stars and sand collapse.
O omnipotent, omniscient, omnivorous

Father in Heaven, let me not be remembered
for the rabid lengths I'll go. I'd go, again.

## KNOWING CHILDREN

It would be nice to believe
that our children hold the future in their hands.
The truth is that the past
grips them even more tightly.

Old grudges settle in their laps
like family dogs: a bitten ear, a slight stench
from the drip of sweet saliva. Our children could never bear
to put them down.

Familiar phrases start turning up
in those tiny mouths with funny teeth,
returning musicality
to the most tired of dogmas.

Freed from concreteness,
history sublimes far above them as another sky—
in its clouds, one child sees the shape of a strawberry.
Another sees a head on a mount.

## DREAM OF GOD AS A VENTURE CAPITALIST

Viewed from space, the world's diverse forms of anguish coalesce
    into a blue tremble—
at least that's how it looked in my dream
in which I was God manipulating levers indiscriminately.
Compassion is more a company slogan, God said.
There were no democracies in my dream, only benevolent
    dictatorships.
The rideshare drivers were all ordained as priests,
disseminating forgiveness to the rain-soaked travelers and drunks.
As God, I knew that when man kneels, it's mostly performative.
I didn't hold that against them.
When, as a kid, I knocked off the head of the angel Gabriel,
reattaching it with hot glue so that whoever bumped it next might
    absorb my punishment,
I could not fathom that there might not be a punishment.
I can fathom it now.
God said the numbers look good.
We're projecting expansion.
Worshippers smiled as meteorites lit up the terror-vaulted sky.
The air brightened and warmed.
I told them they'd be blessed this year greatly.
I told them it was a sign.

## ANTI-ODE TO THE METAPHYSICAL

It's an easy thing to complain.
Watch me do it
there by rock formations older than any government.

There, beneath trees shivering with crows.
It's so easy I can do it underwater
not even knowing how to swim.

It's easier than falling in love
and, truthfully, is as tender.
In the morning,

nestlings chirp with hunger.
In the night, crickets whine
to be loved.

I've heard rumors of a greater being
whose whole purpose is to field
our questions.

Well, this is not so much a question
as it is a comment, and not so much a comment
as it is a critique.

My ailing body refutes the summer's songs.
I've lost no more than the average man,
but no less, either.

Steeped in patriotism, my children
grow entitled to and estranged from the world.
Trouble enough, this ephemeral life.

Eternity?
Well, I can already tell you
how that will go.

## THE GHOSTS OF MY PAST ARE IN DISREPAIR

My ghosts are faulty.
They congratulate me on my home loan.
I find refrigerator magnets often arranged as words of
	encouragement:
*GREAT JOB, KEEP IT UP CHAMP*, etc.
At night, I plug my ears beneath the covers, yet still I can hear them
	bragging about their
children's, grandchildren's, great-great-grandchildren's salaries.
Life has a limited supply of graces to offer,
and I admit to squandering mine,
but they apologize for their part in my transgressions
instead of holding me to account.
I inherited my grandfather's grim outlook and his father's
	impulsivity, they explain.
But your blood pressure, they caution.
But your intentions, they affirm.
It's a widespread problem.
I wrote a letter of complaint to the authorities, my ghosts peering
	over my shoulder, nodding their heads,
saying, *Such masterful syntax!*
saying, *Such tasteful imagery!*
saying, *Your voice, so necessary and brave!*

## LIVING IN THE MOMENT

I like to live
      in the moment. No,
not that one—

not the moment I, knowing perfectly well where he was,

lied to my mother for my father's sake.

Not the one when I realized

the injured heron I had helped into a cage,
                    nursed amateurishly,
might have been better off without me—

not the one in which happiness
                    turned out to be ignorance,
          and charity
                    turned out to be arrogance.

I like to live in moments like this one:
                    a toilet flushing
                    in the upstairs apartment,
                    moths tapping at the lamplit window.

          I am alone

and can hear my neighbor humming
through poorly insulated walls.

In a moment such as this,
          what is joy but infinite?
                    What is consequence
but merely an odor wafting in from the outside world?

                    What a wonderful thing
Solitude is, full of excuses—
          I mean beauty.

## ALTERNATE ENDING: THE INVENTION OF SCIENCE

The serpent reports back to Adam outside the Garden.
*It's not for you to understand*, Adam says, before

cutting that loose end. Already, mortality tills away
at his joints. But this is what he wanted.

Power requires, he realized in his boredom, scarcity.
The figs and chamomile. The meat of a frog.

Only now can he, with God's back facing him,
claim ownership. His desire for Eve, uncurated,

tilts toward lust. Eve, guilt-fed, reaches
for his hand. He grabs her wrist.

The first sob of grief emerges awkwardly from her mouth;
Adam investigates, attempting to understand

what he never thought to name: *glottis, uvula*.
Against death, detail might now be a necessary thing.

## REASONS TO DESPISE BEING LITERARY

You know exactly the caliber of human being
you're not. The birds are old news in the docket
of the beautiful. You jot inconsequential notes:
The Spanish *morir* recalls the English more.
A slant-rhyme: *serenaded to*; *serrated tooth*.
You know that, as Keats died, he did so in the throes
of unrelenting failure. Your apologies are too well-crafted,
and so read as insincere. You insist the oceans swell
like fluid in the skull, but the only person listening
already agrees. When two mirrors face each other,
the image bounces at light speed, shrinks into pure calculation.
Amazing!—but outside your expertise. There's a taste
of ruin in the air that you're convinced has waited centuries
for an articulation only you could orchestrate.
You continue to believe this into the last decade of your life.
Like a machinist who has come to terms with their outdatedness,
you recline staring upwards into that great, blue depth.
Only the naïve call it the firmament.
All you can offer anyone suffering in the world
is a sentence, which is more often than not not enough.

## THE FAMILY ENDURES MAGRITTE'S REVISIONS OF
## *LA CHAMBRE D'ÉCOUTE*

Filled today by a giant apple. The day before,
a black-winged fish. Once the skull of a reptile

that gave the children nightmares. Once, pure
absence, which was difficult to comprehend.

Twice, a haystack; the first we hauled out
in wheelbarrows, but after the last bale,

another haystack. A priest claimed
cosmic superposition; one physicist thought

God. In the kitchen, as I wipe plates
and set them in the rack, I hear crows flutter

as they gather in our strangest room. My children
shout, throwing handfuls of apple meat.

Perhaps tomorrow, it will be a bathtub of our own ashes
or two starved wolverines in a birdcage.

But today, we have this apple:
something close enough to call a gift.

## HOW TO CONFRONT THE PAST

You take the knife of epistemology and the elegiac fork. You comb
the bones from your hair. You imagine yourself appointed president
emeritus of your sins. You stockpile funerals. The animatronic
rendering of your first marriage is less flattering than you would
have liked. One robotic iteration of you slams the table. Another
listens only to itself. You ignore any nuance in favor of horror and
romance. You lance the abscess. You stitch the eyelid shut. You
hound and you bird and you serpent. You cherry-pick one moment:
a child in the woods behind a warehouse where you clawed out
channels through which rainwater flowed. You fossilize this sweet-
ness. You convert time into uninsured damage. You convert time
into white sheets clinging to your sweat. You converse with Time,
whose advice never changes. Who only ever says, *Forget*.

## ERIK ESTRADA DEFENDS HIS PLACE IN THE CANON

See, back then, Latinos were served only with a side of pocket-
    knives—
hair greased sharp as black letter print. Back then,
Spanish Harlem stank of stray dogs and gasoline.
Back then, I sold snow cones with my grandfather
and learned to shortchange. I wasn't raised to be a beauty.
Back then, my mother's Spanish moved about the house
like a ghost only she could see.
Back when I knew what was good for me,
the stage ached for my foot to grace it.
I played criminal. I played and became police.
Then, I was the question to an answer on *Jeopardy*.
Then, I saw my reflection in the teeth of John Wayne.
The term "trailblazer" had been applied.
Even my arms had their own scenes—when Hollywood
drank the exhaust of my motorcycle, and my dark
skin lit up the screen: small and silver.
In Reagan's America, I was celebrated,
the Puerto Rican in every Mexican American's heart.
Politics evolve, but I stay put, badge sparkling.
The shifting landscape can't move a star.
Back when my father left us—back then, I knew
I'd be a man whose very presence was his art.

## INTELLIGENT DESIGN

An engineer in Wisconsin claims to have improved grief's design.
*Aerodynamic*, he says, showing off his sketches, *barely grief at all!*
Applying physics like salve to a wound, he remembers what Torricel-
li said about vacuums, what Carnot said about absolute terror. He
grabs a pencil and revises one more time. *There's money to be made
in this*, his father would assure, chopping chicken-necks through
the afternoon. Flightless birds! The engineer pores over schematics,
grimaces at draft after draft. His last sketch: confused. Joints
unlabeled. A room inside a room inside a room.

## EROSION

A star fantasizes about darkness. A child fantasizes about the gold earrings of her teacher, who tells her stars outlast us all. God fantasizes about time, which, even after all His experimenting, He fails to grasp completely. The earrings, shaped like golden orbits, sway as she nods. Gravity cannot stop fantasizing about cosmic bodies. A rock, released by the child into the air above a river, fears erosion, but also finds it vaguely erotic. A rock is one of the smallest bodies gravity fantasizes about. Smaller, still: a grain of sand. The shore's morals are eroding, the sand knows. Lying on the shore, composing it, the grain of sand recalls the flirtations of cartographers and how maps grow more beautiful in the dark.

## -ISM

In the eternal tussle for beauty
between concrete and abstract,
tonight I side with the abstract.

I posit the dandelions in the yard
as a yard's dandelionism,
I miss the forest for the fractals
of its branches.

Sidestepping the mystics,
I embrace the mysticism.

There are so many answers to choose from
in the orchard of the immaterial.
I eat its fruit: not emptiness, but emptihood
one learns to share with others.

Not loneliness.

Each of life's gifts, unwrapped,
is full of contradiction—
*against-speech*, not *against speech*,
*against* the way light,
each evening, breaks against the water,

the way my dull routines ricochet against
the arc of time.

Or contradictions that have no shape
or sound, only meaning,

only meaning, which carries me forward
the way a bird carries that writhing serpent
who senses, for the first time,

a great expanse.

## FALSE COGNATES

When I learned there was more
than one language, I raised a finger to my tongue

in wonder. When I learned there was more
than one language, my neck warmed

from embarrassment. My parents had kept secrets.
I began to suspect everything of withholding

idiom: outside, trees would shiver codes
in long shadows; kitchen knives would glint sequences

when held. A boy understands most what he touches.
I heard *cielo* and pictured a horsehair bow across taut strings.

*Luz* was the verb for all that was and would be taken.

My children have yet to tongue the empty space
in their mouths—that special gap histories fall out of.

Their cavities of singing. Their cavity *singular.*

## SPEAKING ILL OF THE DEAD

Chasing a specter of survival,
my grandmother visited a small church
near the Rio Grande rumored to heal.
Inside, the walls were adorned
with canonical paintings:
*The Sacred Heart; Our Lady of Guadalupe*—
images my grandmother prayed before
when she discovered she was pregnant
with my mother at thirteen.
Instructed by her elders to sacrifice
for the other life in her otherwise empty
belly, she prayed through her doubt.
The chapel mostly empty as morning light
seeped through stained glass,
she set her sequined purse on a pew
and prostrated herself before the altar.
Terrified. My sister played with her dolls.
I cut verses from the hymnal book
with cosmetic scissors. Even then,
beseeching a god she was beginning to fear
had abandoned her, or, even worse,
had been a figment all along, she said
not one gentle thing. As she died,
her last words were to my mother.

*I tried, I tried,* she whined,
*I'm sorry I could never love you.*

My mother forgave her those words,
keeps them close to her—
a keepsake I could never fathom.
She says it's comforting, it's comforting
to know she tried.

## ELEGY WITH NO TENOR

What can I do
but run,

one foot after the other,
toward metaphor.

I move my hand toward
a light bulb in the dark.

As my hand gets closer,
I can feel residual warmth.

There used to be.
There was once.

There now is.

## ELONGATIONS

When my mother says that faith alone
                saved her from suicide, which she first said

when we were alone in the timeless space
                of my bedridden recovery from a flu,

what she means is that, like the guitar
                I practiced in front of her, what's hollowed out

resonates with a kind of beauty that is all
                departure, an exhalation of sound called *song*.

She means that, at the table set for children
                who share her fear of their father's return,

the buzzing is not the ceiling fan's rusted motor,
                but that of her god working from body to body,

tightening rivets in rattled souls. I, who listen
                faithfully as she mourns again her stolen youth,

her forced marriage that never stopped devising
                new instruments of degradation, understand that

even in listening, I've become an organ of that cruelty,
                a beloved elongation of her sharpest griefs.

This is what I learned of love—

an intimacy with the injury inflicted in its name.
                Sure, there's beauty. There's warmth.

But like a winter garden's, it's in the soil—
                it's the warmth of decay.

## THE VESTIGIAL

Survival can be its own affliction.

Wings that do not lift the body
become merely weight.

The recessed orifice of a luna moth's
mouth limits its life span to seven days.

Even a body of knowledge
is shaped this way.

In the soft tissue of my country,
empire has calcified
into the smallest habits:

a hat removed for an anthem;
a trigger finger whitening at each flexed joint.

The arc of history bends
but won't break.

Gracefully, the moth brushes nectar
with the covering of its mouth
and dies hungry,

having secured its eggs
to my potted fronds.

## THE UNTRANSLATABLE

On the hatched
 egg's center. I
lightly press
 my finger.
Spiderlings with
 legs thinner
than hairs.
 Spiral up
my knuckle.
 Some leap
off, catching
 a gust of    wind.
With silk.
 Two blocks away,
one car speeds
 into another.
A metallic
 consonant    echoes.
Through pines,
 and birds.
Struck by
 this language.

Coo back to it.

# THE APHIDS

So that a blue jay might take notice
of the easy meal, my brothers taped a
lizard to an oak tree. After a short
hunt, they had caught it by its tail,
which snapped off, and caught it
again, pinching its neck in the dirt,
then held it up: on its white belly, a
small drop of piss trembled, catch-
ing brilliantly the glare of noon. Its
eyelids closed shut, pale rim to pale
rim. I raked insects from the grass to
hand-feed it, and when it refused to
open its mouth, I forced its mouth
open. My brothers, the little terrors
of the neighborhood, waited quietly
for nature's stroke of white gore
and blue grace, planting themselves
among hibiscus, their dark hair
disappearing within a nearly flagrant
red. As the yard grew darker, I joined
them in the stalks. I sat long enough
to ask questions, but asked none.
Beside me, aphids tapped their legs
on each other's bodies, and I thought
they must be speaking through touch.

## ASTROPHYSICS

In the vacuum of space, each prayer
                     is swallowed like dishwater.

I do not tell my daughter this
                     as she prays for snow.

The winter sky—winter
                     because of orbital alignments and axes—

purples above us. White noise
                     falling over him like snow, Christ

feared his father's silence in the end.
                     Most of the known universe consists

of misalignment: more is being destroyed
                     now than ever before. My daughter

nicks her ear on a kitchen drawer.
                     I apply pressure with a duck-print cloth.

Red blooms through yellow—a first duck,
                     then a second. Some nights, we read

from her favorite astronomy book.
                     I struggle to explain the difference

between bodies and dust.

## ALTERNATE ENDING: THE ESCAPE OF JEPHTHAH'S DAUGHTER

Seeing my father tear his clothes at the sight of me,
each seam of cloth unspindling to reveal his bare,

flexing chest as he wailed a heartfelt regret,
I could no longer take him seriously. God,

I realized, played favorites and favored fools.
Who did he think would walk through the door

to greet him? *The irony!*—I could hear the future
exclaim. *And a virgin sacrifice, at that!*

But I'm no archetype. I fled to the mountains,
promising return, but what is a promise if not

an exchange of ideas about ourselves, subject
to evolving circumstances? If my nation burns, so be it.

Many will be grateful. And there's no lack of men
eager to sing of how they suffered greatly and prevailed.

## MEDITATION ON THE LAST PRAYER

When the hands fold,

darkness forms

like a conversation

between them.

## THE INTERVAL

*Some Assembly Required*, reads the box
of my daughter's dollhouse, which sits
in the garage years after its purchase.

One gives up on things, like the idea
of being the father you wish you had.

My daughter, whom I see alternating
weekends, loves hearing shuffle blues
on Sunday mornings, which I play for her

on my guitar while she relevés and headbangs
across the den, not yet discriminating genre.

I know there's a well of resentment somewhere,
not yet tapped. But, in this moment, I only
need to keep time: the Eb, the Ab, the Bb,

the flat-tire rhythm of a song that, for now,
is absent words.

When the music ends,

there's a moment of silence, or almost-silence,
as her feet tap the floor, dancing anyway.

## PASTORAL

The cows chewing on the field grass have only
a partial belief in god. Their belief in god resembles
my belief in my own goodness, a vaguely present thing.

The flies that hang around their asses disperse
when the cows flinch, and gather again.
I've been told terrible things about the impact

of my words. I try to use them more carefully
as I grow older, ridiculing others only to myself.
I try to mete out what mercy I've been allotted.

It's hard not to admire the tranquility of these cows
that buckle their legs beneath the shade of ash trees
while listening to the distant snaps of machinery

invented to ease the slaughter. I was young.
I may still be. I hurt people I loved, and I believed
in forgiveness as one of the many laws of nature

on my side.

## A MAN'S APOLOGY

I never heard the words from my father.
If you can imagine a slug
on a scrap of driftwood
in the middle of the Dead Sea,

that's his position on the subject.
Let's not talk about it.
Let's ferry our bitterness a little further.
In the waters, calm and saline,

two men embrace, think the words,
and sink. They share one
of the three kinds of silence:
silence toward the familiar.

Colder is the silence
toward that which makes us feel
estranged. I try to remember
which of my father's silences

tucked me in at night.
I wouldn't call it distant.
I could feel its warmth
like a breath down my neck

turning each square inch
of skin to stone.
Sons make beautiful monuments.
I know because I am the father now,

shaping a life that I hope
might float on water—
but it's the emptiness in a thing
that makes it buoyant.

Let's not talk about it.
Let's keep waiting for forgiveness
to arrive like a late tide over which we have,
after all, such little influence.

Anger swells.
Why not forgiveness, too?

## THE WORD

God complains that the angels have become nihilists. *Sure*, He says, *they'll herald, but only apocalyptic news. They instill maddening images in the minds of My prophets: birds flying toward erasure; moons eating moons.* On barstools cast in gold, God and I sit, shaking our heads. Annihilated by His presence, I'm resurrected again and again. He sighs, animating the ice cubes in His glass. He utters a word, and the angels all vanish. The flirty bartender vanishes. The belly of time distends. *All I've ever wanted*, He says, *is a creature that fears me and calls it love.*

## MEDITATION ON BEAUTY

There are days I think beauty has been exhausted.
Then, I read about the New York subway cars

dumped into the ocean to replace dying reefs.
Coral gilds the stanchions, feathered with dim Atlantic light.

Fish glisten, darting through a window into the sea grass
that bends around them like green flames—

this is human-enabled grace. Maybe there's room
in the margin of error for us to save ourselves

from trends of self-destruction. Or maybe beauty
is just another distraction. We stuff our hearts

with its currency and parade for applause.
Here, in the South, I can hear applause coming

from the ground. Even the buried are divided.
At the bottom of the Gulf, dark with Mississippi silt,

rests the broken derrick of an oil rig—and isn't oil
beautiful? More ancient and opaque than the allegories

suggesting that we sacrifice our most beloved. Likely
ourselves. In one photograph, a sea turtle skims its belly

across a hull, unimpressed with what's restored,
barely aware of the ocean around it growing warm.

## THE BURNING FIELD

1. Drought

I thought of each prayer as a pocket of air
in which God resided:

grief-boats wisping across
the vague architecture of a fever dream—

animals fled.

My mother prayed
each morning before her children stirred.

Our park's grass turned fawn and crackled as it was tread,

the grassfires spreading closer
to our home. I remember a charred house

along the highway—such privacy
reduced to something skeletal, exhibitionist.

It was easy to put our faith in the drought,
in its everlastingness, in the way
it punished alike the unjust and the just.


2. Arson

Two boys started a forest fire in Tennessee.
It approached a woman's house the way a man

might—with no intention of harm.

The only thing she chose to save were the ashes of her father,
collected in an aluminum vase painted the shade of red
his palms took in winter.

I think about her fear often—
that his ashes might be subsumed,
how she protected the singularity of her pain.

One boy's mother said

to his father: *See? This is what I've been telling you* ...

The other boy's mother expressed disbelief
that the light in her son's eyes needed just
a little tinder; horror settled tenderly in her heart

as ash. Still, she prays for her son:

*And fire came down from God*
*out of heaven and devoured them.*

*And the God who answers by fire—He is God.*


3. Controlled Burn

No one tells the field animals it's prescribed.
No one tells the spiders, as their carapaces

crackle in the flames like a strange tinnitus,
that things are under control. Flames travel

opposite to water, licking up hills and trees,
as if attempting escape—or return, the plume

of smoke a black feather dropped from God's wings.
I know my own mouth's cruelty.

I felt the weapon of prayer pressed on my tongue.
Cinders float in the distance: orange alphabet

arranging a verse of scripture too ephemeral
to read. My mother licks her thumb and turns

to Revelations, her favorite book, where God
admits to a love she can recognize,
a love like other men's,

                    absolutist, obliterating.

## A FORCE EQUAL TO THE WEIGHT OF THE FLUID DISPLACED

*In August 2017, Hurricane Harvey caused massive flooding in the Gulf Coast region, taking over a hundred lives, and displacing tens of thousands. While many suffered great loss, those affected most were those already economically vulnerable.*

1.

From the brute                    sky fell

          a precipitation

of names onto                  rooftops. Names

          filling our ditches

overnight.                        I tilted my head

          and caught one

on my tongue                  where it remains—I try

          to speak

but can form                    no other sound.

          I say it

in anger,                        in grief.

          In exhaustion.

I'm not alone—               all of us lost

          to recitation.

2.

In the second of three dreams one night,
a white dress churned downstream.
In the third of three dreams, my two children
opened their small hands, pouring fire ants
into the oleaginous waters at their ankles.
Ants clung together until a red island formed;
its red sand climbed our naked legs; its red
trees bore red fruit that dispersed across
our swelling hands that couldn't help
but pluck it. I woke to a thin weatherman
sweating through his grey suit, highlighting
cell after rotating cell, my county's name
flashing across the bottom of the screen.
It was my watch that night. I checked
the yard. I checked the garage. My fingers
tapping on the couch's fabric, I weighed
whom among my neighbors I *could* help
against whom I *would*, invented rubrics
they passed or failed—calculations
that never leave a mind forced to make them,
like a sediment after the rains. I check again.

3.

The rains pause. A lingering current, dark as myrrh,
makes heavy all it touches. Walls, brushed by its silt lips,
decay. Mosquito eggs embedded in the house's fabrics
are too small to remove. Emergency lights flicker
on the crest of a small wave as it approaches the door,
a truck or boat having passed. Unseen in tall grasses,
frogs inflame the air with noise. Sleep is thin; one slips
into it disquietly. Omnipresent is the sky's whisper

against us. I heard reports of a flooded house
that caught flame. Nothing could be done. The task
of salvation dissipates like the embers that fell
onto the water and debris with an evanescent hiss.
Gone. Away is water's preposition; it doesn't ask
how far. Far enough. Too far? Who can tell.

4.

| | | |
|---|---|---|
| Petrochemicals | Oceanic temperature | Feeder band |
| Communion dress | Fecal Matter | Shelter |
| Deportation | Mating calls | Sediment |
| Breach | Rotating cell | White van |
| Capsize | Prayer | Controlled release |
| Buoyancy | Pocket of sky | Pocket of earth |
| Environmental racism | Boil order | Rain |
| Lung capacity | Rain | Rain |
| Rain | Rain | Rain |

5.

In the first dream, a song was playing from a car half-submerged.
No, that wasn't a dream.


In the first dream, no one was baptized.


On white bedsheets strapped to rooftops were written epistles to
God. *Dear God*, one said, *your fever is climbing. Dear God, could you
pause for a moment and think?*


To fit one's life in a Glad trash bag is a peculiar ritual, noted
some men in my first dream.


Before my first dream, the weatherman stumbled neatly over his
words, his syntax unfolding like a ladder down which I climbed into
sleep.


In the first dream, rain became the sound of breathing, proto-
language, a rising inflection none of us could sustain.

## THE MAKER

God gives you a needle, a feather, and a rope. The rope was a mistake. When you mistook the feather for a metaphor, you were embarrassed. *My child*, God said to you, *be content*. God gives you a swastika divorced from history. He gives you data inconsistent with the observed. God gives you a song, and your entire life you spend revising it. *At its core*, God says to you, *it has not changed*. No longer immutable, God gives you forgiveness. No longer God, he flirts and buys you a round. You take the round and load it into a rifle. *God, you ask, can't I go back to the needle and the metaphor?* He insists you not romanticize the past. God gives you bloodstream, bones, and loneliness. He extracts impurities lingering in the soul. *I am first and foremost a scientist*, God explains to you, *heavyhearted and with primitive tools*.

## ALTERNATE BEGINNING: THE SIXTH DAY

On the sixth day, God said, *On second thought,*
*man's flightlessness presents a problem—*

*seeing narrowly what's in front. Perhaps birds*
*should be in charge.* He tinkered anatomically,

sliding His tongue across His teeth. Dissatisfied,
He considered how no animal is tenderer than

the Weddell seal—though what makes a steward
if not the wisdom of the octopus? Being made

in His image, turns out, comes with unexpected kinks.
He labored into the newly invented evening,

time perspiring as opals on His brow. He thought
about all His previous universes that had failed.

His seven hundred and twelfth was His favorite,
with its beaches of embers and aphotic darkness.

*What if there is no right animal,* God pondered,
His coronal eye wandering to another kingdom:

*The lichen!*—dialectic flower whose symbiosis
perfects a thesis of communion! *Rock tripe.*

*Moonglow. Witch's hair. Shield. Script. Chalice.*

## PLACES WITH TERRIBLE WI-FI

The Garden of Eden. My ancestors' graves. A watermelon field in Central Texas where my father once slept. Miles of rivers. The waiting room of a hospital in which a doctor, thin-looking in his coat, shared mixed results. A den of worms beneath the frozen grass. Jesus's tomb. The stretches of highway on the long drive home after burial. The figurative abyss. The literal heavens. The cheap motel room in which I thought about praying despite my disbelief. What I thought was a voice was simply a recording playing from another room. The cluttered attic. Most of the past. The very distant future, where man is just another stratum in the ground. The Tel of Megiddo. The flooded house and the scorched one. My favorite cemetery, where I can touch the white noise distorting memory. What is static if not the sound of the universe's grief? Anywhere static reigns.

## STATIC

One great metaphor can ruin a life. And we have invented several:
the borne fruit, the eternal battle between darkness and light.
Geometricians of the ancient world grappled with the difference
between two names and two names within a circle.
In his phone conversation, a father spoke of how, after he left,
he would brush his teeth in the dark. As if it were anything more
than photons bouncing back at him. Sometimes, a word must
    be fabricated
from its brass and bloodshed. Sometimes, just its utterance fractures
dinnerware left for another to wash. Solar winds in the atmosphere
fill the phone conversation with static. Airwaves alight with genesis—
a fraction of what interrupts coinciding with creation itself.
*My father,* I say to him, *can't you see you are a figment*
*in someone's dark imagination. My father, turn on the lights*
*and realize that you're alone.* He rolls an orange across grass yellowing
from the shade of gardenias. He lays a jackal inside a burning bassinet.

## IN PRAISE OF WEAKNESS

When my son
grips my hand,

I am touched
with what

my father feared—
that weakness

tingling first
in my knuckles,

then flaming
through my chest.

All the ways
in which I might

fail him
populate the charted

territory. A point
of pride for my father:

how his finger
never bent

when pressed
against my chest.

As my thumb
wipes the milk

from my son's lips,
I think of

my father's lips.
Always closed.

Never parting
to say the words.

I say the words.
I say them again:

the words
that will survive me.

## AT LAST, SURRENDER

Sanding the drywall of a house behind schedule,
a man across the street calls out to his son who jumps

on a roll of unused chain-link in the front lawn.
The windows begin to brighten as evening rarefies

light. White dust sheds from walls with each stroke
of his sanding pole. It catches, I know, on hairs

all across the body, some specks settling in the lungs:
fine irritants. After work, my father would track it

into the house and shake it from his thinning hair,
its texture on my tongue dryer than chalk.

Once, he took me to a jobsite far from the city,
where night erased every detail of the woods—

the kind of darkness that reaches into memory,
seeking light to swallow. Inside, all the windows

became mirrors, and, looking into one, I studied him
sanding the walls, the papery timbre and even rhythm.

Dust fell around us like the debris of our shared ghosts.
Heading home on a country-dark road, our headlights

rendered a small fraction of the world. Our tires
upheaved dirt, glowing red. He switched off the radio

when the signal faltered and rolled both windows down,
engine noise swelling as we passed each thicket of trees,

our silence nearly a religious one—
we borrowed gentleness and couldn't speak.

## ACKNOWLEDGMENTS

My gratitude to the readers and editors of the following publications, in which these poems or their earlier versions, first appeared:
*Bennington Review*: "Places with Terrible Wi-Fi"
*Boston Review*: "The Maker"
*The BreakBeat Poets Vol. 4: LatiNEXT*: "Pastoral," "My Uncle's Killer," also reprinted in *POETRY*
*The Iowa Review*: "Independence Day in West Texas"
*Horsethief Magazine*: "How to Confront the Past"
*Meridian*: "Astrophysics" and "Intelligent Design"
*Mid-American Review*: "The Politics of Rivers"
*Michigan Quarterly Review*: "Elegy with No Tenor," originally printed as "The Figurative"
*Ninth Letter*: "Static"
*Ploughshares*: "Theodicy Written in the Occupied Sands"
*The New Yorker*: "Meditation on Beauty," also reprinted in *The Compact Bedford Introduction to Literature, 12th Ed.*, and "Erik Estrada Defends His Place in the Canon"
*The Shallow Ends*: "A Metaphor"
*TriQuarterly*: "The Contract"
*Waxwing*: "False Cognates"
*s*: "The Burning Field"

Thank you to the friends and mentors who helped me with the earliest versions of this manuscript, including Kaveh Akbar, Brooks Haxton, Cynthia Dewi Oka, Matthew Olzmann, Kevin Prufer, and Martha Rhoades.

Thank you to the friends and mentors who have supported and heartened me on this long journey, including Hannah Aizenman, Debra Allbery, Eloisa Amezcua, Michael Anna de Armas, Sarah Audsley, Rachel Beeton, Erika Jo Brown, Cortney Lamar Charleston, Benjamin Garcia, Joshua Gottlieb-Miller, Roy G. Guzmán, Perry Janes, Rodney Jones, Ada Limón, Ricardo Alberto Maldonado, Lupe Mendez, Angel Nafis, Hieu Minh Nguyen, Joseph Nieves, José Olivarez, Daniel Peña, Megan Pinto, Ben Purkert, Margaret Ray, Iliana Rocha, Mallory Rodenberg, Laurie Rosenblatt, Analicia Sotelo, Kristen Sahaana Surya, Vanessa Angélica Villareal, Bryan Washington, and countless others with whom I have been lucky to cross paths.

Thank you to following organizations: Inprint Houston, The Slow-down Podcast, Tintero Projects, and the Warren Wilson College MFA Program for Writers.

Thank you to Carey Salerno, Alyssa Neptune, and everyone at Alice James Books for helping to bring this book into the world.

And the deepest gratitude goes to my family. To my mom, Dorothy. To my partner, Astacia. And to my children, Juniper, Harry, and Imelda. I would be lost without you.

## RECENT TITLES FROM ALICE JAMES BOOKS

Alice James Books is committed to publishing books that matter. The press was founded in 1973 in Boston, Massachusetts as a co-operative, wherein authors performed the day-to-day undertakings of the press. This element remains present today, as authors who publish with the press are invited to collaborate closely in the publication process of their work. AJB remains committed to its founders' original feminist mission, while expanding upon the scope to include all voices and poets who might otherwise go unheard. In keeping with its efforts to build equity and increase inclusivity in publishing and the literary arts, AJB seeks out poets whose writing possesses the range, depth, and ability to cultivate empathy in our world and to dynamically push against silence. The press was named for Alice James, sister to William and Henry, whose extraordinary gift for writing went unrecognized during her lifetime.

Designed by Francine Kass
Printed by McNaughton & Gunn